'Liz's succinct and practi.   reference
accessible to all teaching
sitting to give an informed
book to aid support with ev   classroom issues. Deep
yet accessible, this is a must-read for all those who are
embarking on a teaching or teacher support career.'

– Viv Formby, retired headteacher

'As a Special Educational Needs Coordinator I find this
book invaluable. The book is short enough for profes-
sionals to read quickly in its entirety. It is full of good
suggestions which in my experience will actually make a
difference. I can't recommend it enough.'

– Be Rimmer, Primary Special
Educational Needs Coordinator

'A thoroughly worthwhile read that should be on all teacher
training essential book lists. It provides no-nonsense, to-
the-point advice for all teachers, but especially for those
who are new to teaching. The advice in this book could
take a career to learn and master, yet is here for the taking.
It's excellent value for money and time – far cheaper
than a course! This is a positive and practical approach
to behaviour management based on tried-and-tested
experience and wisdom. It has excellent advice for setting
up a classroom and managing behaviour on a daily basis
within it. Even after 30 years of teaching, I still learned
some new strategies by reading this book.'

– Alison Albion, Headteacher at
WLSJ CE Primary School, Lancashire

'At a time when we are being told that there is a worrying increase in the number of young people and children reporting and being identified as having mental health problems, Liz William's book comes as a highly accessible and practical guide designed to help staff in primary schools to understand the importance of promoting resilience and social and emotional wellbeing in young children. Without becoming explicitly technical, the book draws on a range of underlying theories and approaches, taking a practical "what works" approach that is likely to be welcomed in schools. Great for beginners and those with less experience, and for those in search of a quick prompt or reminder.'

– *Chris Watkinson, Educational Psychologist*

Positive Behaviour Management in Primary Schools

by the same author

Positive Behaviour Management in Early Years Settings
An Essential Guide
ISBN 978 1 78592 026 4
eISBN 978 1 78450 273 7

of related interest

Building Positive Momentum for Positive Behavior in Young Children
Strategies for Success in School and Beyond
Lisa Rogers
ISBN 978 1 78592 774 4
eISBN 978 1 78450 679 7

Creating Excellence in Primary School Playtimes
How to Make 20% of the School Day 100% Better
Michael Follett
ISBN 978 1 78592 098 1
eISBN 978 1 78450 361 1

A Kit Bag for Promoting Positive Behaviour in the Classroom
Nicola S. Morgan and Gillian Ellis
ISBN 978 1 84905 213 9
eISBN 978 0 85700 466 6

Positive Behaviour Management in Primary Schools

AN ESSENTIAL GUIDE
Liz Williams

Jessica Kingsley *Publishers*
London and Philadelphia

First published in 2018
by Jessica Kingsley Publishers
73 Collier Street
London N1 9BE, UK
and
400 Market Street, Suite 400
Philadelphia, PA 19106, USA

www.jkp.com

Library of Congress Cataloging in Publication Data
A CIP catalog record for this book is available
from the Library of Congress

British Library Cataloguing in Publication Data
A CIP catalogue record for this book is available from the British Library

ISBN 978 1 78592 361 6
eISBN 978 1 78450 704 6

Printed and bound in the Great Britain

MIX
Paper from
responsible sources
FSC® C013056

To Keith, Emma and Laura

Acknowledgements

In memory of Marion Bennathan OBE, 29 May 1927 – 4 February 2018, Honorary Life President of the Nurture Group Network and Honorary Director of Young Minds, who shaped the way I thought and the direction in which I took the services that I ran.

Contents

Introduction

Developing children's social, emotional and behavioural skills can sometimes be challenging for staff in schools. The term 'behaviour' itself can be emotive since we all have our own understanding of what the word means and we all have behaviours that we find more or less acceptable within a given context. Helping children to develop these skills can be brought about more easily by considering a number of factors. The term 'behaviour management' is not necessarily a popular term, but it is frequently used and, I would argue, still very relevant – as long as you see it in its broadest terms and acknowledge that it is more often than not the adults who have to manage their own behaviour while supporting children to develop their skills.

Having worked with schools over many years, it became apparent to me that I was being asked the same questions over and over again with regard to behaviour management and that most schools in effect needed similar advice. This is not to say in any way that each school is the same and that children's situations and circumstances are not unique; rather that the starting points for teaching the skills children may need seem to be broadly similar. The systems in the end will most probably turn out to be different, as all behaviour happens in a context and is dependent on many factors, including relationships.

This book is designed to be a quick guide, maybe for beginners and those with less experience, those who have just qualified or are learning to teach, and also maybe for those of us who have been working in the field for years and who would just like to have a quick refresher. All of us are lifelong learners, so no matter what our experience and background, we can always hone our skills and understanding.

Everything in this book is offered for consideration, to be mulled over and to be tested out. In this field there are no firm and fast answers, but there are systems, structures, techniques and approaches that can be of use to staff, parents and children alike. Some of these suggestions and approaches may seem overly simplistic, but they are grounded in research – in evidence of what has been seen to work – and pull together my findings over at least 20 years.

The chapter headings give an indication of the scope of the book. The book has been kept deliberately short so that it can be read quickly in its entirety, and that is really the way in which I would prefer you to view it; however, the headings are there so that you can have an even quicker look at any particular section if you so wish.

The material in each section should set the reader off in the right direction, in terms of mindset and actions, and is intended as a starting point. The book is written in uncomplicated language in order to make it accessible and user-friendly.

It is important to remember that none of us have the 'answers', but it's the will to support children and develop their skills that counts. This often requires developing our own skills at the same time!

I would welcome any feedback, and thank you for taking a look.

Liz Williams
www.lizwilliamsconsultancy.co.uk

1

Definitions of Behaviour

The first question is 'What do we mean by behaviour?' Behaviour can be defined as the way in which one acts or conducts oneself, especially towards others, the way in which a person behaves in response to a particular situation, the way we go about things. But it's actually a bit more complex than that.

When behaviour is mentioned in the context of children in schools, all too often it is because children are not behaving in a way that adults want or like. In other words, the behaviour is negative. There is a perception that this behaviour needs to be 'managed' – hence the title of this book. Turn this into a positive; look at behaviour as a set of skills to be learned and applied in a variety of different situations. This is really the key: look for the positives and build on them.

When we focus on the problems and consider negatives, it doesn't really move us on. It is easier to see children's behaviour as simply what they do, how they act and, for staff in schools, what we observe. Children's behaviour isn't actually something we should 'manage'; it's a set of skills and competencies that we should strive to help develop. This includes both 'acting out' behaviour and quiet, withdrawn behaviour. This also includes behaviours that come about due to the presence of a special educational need, where it is important to take learning needs and social and emotional needs together. Children begin to learn skills from the minute they are born. In a group of 25 children there are 25 different skill sets, thought patterns, emotions and background influences. All these things have been learned in different ways and at different times, and there are many things still to be developed.

Children who find it difficult to conform in schools for whatever reason have always been around, but over the years the education system has changed, and in many ways become increasingly formal, with less play, less exploration, less time to develop fundamental skills. The pressures on the education system itself have increased and there is now a greater emphasis on reaching academic targets. Unless we focus on developing social and emotional skills, attempting to promote well-being and strategies to increase resilience as well as academic skills, we are not developing the whole child. Children who are secure and resilient are better able to learn, so teaching these skills is not a 'waste' of time as there is a positive impact on academic achievement. Historically, children who found it hard to fit in were given different labels; society used to call children who didn't quite fit in with the system 'maladjusted', and there have been various theories about how to support them over time. Now there is a far greater understanding of the different skills children need to learn; that in fact one size does not fit all and therefore there may be a need to adjust our systems in order to include everybody, coupled with a need to give experiences that are required. There is also a far greater acceptance than there was in the past of the fact that different children learn in different ways.

When each of us thinks of 'behaviour', we all have a different picture in our heads. Behaviour is subjective – and happens in a particular situation – with various factors influencing it. My definition of 'good' behaviour may not be yours; it's based on what I find acceptable depending on the situation. Likewise, 'inappropriate behaviour': you may find something inappropriate, but I may think that this is fine given the circumstances. The behaviours that I find acceptable in various contexts come from the way I was brought up, my core beliefs and the experiences I have had. It is the same for every individual working with children; although we are likely to have elements in common, our own reasons for believing this are likely to be slightly different.

The belief that positive behaviour is a set of skills that can be taught, encouraged and supported is central, and our professional practice needs to be fair and not unduly influenced by our own personal values and feelings – as far as this is possible. At times it may be necessary for school staff to take a step back and have a look from the outside.

When schools actively make teaching the skills needed for positive behaviour a priority, there are fewer 'difficulties' to deal with. This may seem obvious, but it is quite often an area that does not receive focus until things start to go wrong. A proactive positive approach works best. Try not to wait for it all to unravel!

2

Why We and Children Behave as We Do

The only behaviour you can change is your own. You can teach skills, create situations and give advice to prompt others, but in the end the only behaviour you can change yourself is the behaviour that belongs to you. Changing your behaviour has an impact on how others behave around you. Try it – do something differently and see what happens. Sometimes it can be as simple as sitting in a different chair in a staff meeting or when watching television with your family. When you arrive in school in the morning, make positive statements to the first three adults you meet (not that I am suggesting you don't do this already!): 'Morning – your hair looks lovely today', 'I like that tie – have I seen it before?', 'Thank you so much for your help with my computer yesterday.' It does make a difference. Don't say anything you don't believe to be true, but watch for changes in adults' behaviour when you point out the positives!

The behaviour of any person, child or adult depends on a number of factors. It is important to understand that behaviour is situational – it always happens within a context. For adults, this may be the context of home, work, social events, etc. – people's behaviour is often subtly different accordingly. Every member of staff in a school brings their whole self to work each day; they bring their worries, anxieties, enthusiasm, happiness – to different degrees at different times. Staff/staff relationships are crucial, as well as staff/child relationships.

Think and reflect

What did you bring with you this morning?

Did you sleep well?

Have you had breakfast?

Are you anxious to get home because there is something on your mind?

Children bring the same sorts of things with them when they arrive at school, and we do not always know what these are. Sometimes children tell us if there is something wrong; at other times they don't. It is very much the same with adults. Some of us get snappy when we are hungry – we get 'hangry'. The snarly, awkward behaviour we see may not be due to the fact that someone has just asked us to do something; it may be because we could do with something to eat – in other words, a step away from the situation itself but having an impact upon it.

Behaviour also depends on age, stage of development and academic, social and emotional capacity. Chronological age does not always correlate with emotional and social age, and is dependent on context. This is really very important to consider and is often overlooked. It is perfectly possible, as an adult, to have a toddler tantrum if the situation arises! If we are honest, most of us will have done this at least once in the past; some of us have done it on a regular basis! Just because a child is seven years old, it doesn't mean that emotionally, in some situations, they won't behave as though they are two years old. Behaviour is not necessarily consistent within the same situations – a person faced with a situation on a 'good' day may manage it well; on a 'bad' day the outcome will be different because of their differing emotional states as the same situation arises. Again, this is important: just because Laura can 'behave' in PE on Monday doesn't mean the same will happen on Wednesday when she is 'hangry'.

Our social, emotional and behavioural capacities may well develop at a different rate to our intellectual capacities, in the same way that our ability to recognise a fronted adverbial may develop at a different rate to our ability to code.

As adults, we generally understand how to behave and react in different situations – what is appropriate, what isn't, what can be followed up later – and we have learned a degree of self-control and are able to behave 'appropriately'. A child's world is so much more immediate. They may have a tendency to just do it, to just react, as their self-regulatory skills are still developing – no matter what their age.

If we are preoccupied or worried, this affects our behaviour, and likewise if we are tired, hungry or thirsty. It's the same for children. More often than not we are unaware of the experiences the children in our class have had between waking up and arriving in our classrooms each morning.

Different children will see the world differently depending on their previous life experiences. Children with special educational needs – which may or may not have been identified – may see the world in yet another different way. For example, children with autistic spectrum disorders (ASD) may find it very difficult to build relationships and may become very distressed if routines are not followed to the letter.

The quality of the experiences children have had and the quality of the relationships they go on to build are crucial. They need consistency; firm but flexible boundaries; opportunities to interact, learn and explore at developmentally appropriate levels; the freedom to make mistakes; love; nurturing; and opportunities to develop a sense of self. These are things that adults who teach children can have an impact upon.

All behaviour is communication. Sometimes, as adults, we may not immediately understand why the child is behaving as they are. Sometimes we may never understand. Even if we don't understand, we can do our best to create the environment and relationships in order for the child to communicate in what may be a more appropriate way. What is the child trying to tell us? It is important that we try to enable children to develop their own sense of right and wrong rather than just to comply with instructions from adults as to how they should behave. The child's behaviour is a way of giving us a message. In a busy classroom this is often hard to unpick, but it is something that can be returned to at a later stage if we go on to analyse the situation a little bit and maybe come back and speak to the child about what happened.

Some of the elements that are thought to influence behaviour are difficult or impossible for a school to change. For example, it is impossible to change birth order and physical differences, and it is hard to change disposition. However, we can have an impact on skills, including social coping skills, the quality of the environment and the motivation of staff to teach skills and build relationships. As adults, we do this best when we are calm and rational, and when we realise that our own behaviour and emotions can have a huge influence.

It is important to realise that whether or not a child has a 'behaviour difficulty' or a 'behavioural need' is not a fact. It is a belief of the adults associated with the child, based on their personal constructs and their understanding of socially defined criteria.

3

The Importance of Expectations and Teaching Positive Behaviour

As with anything, if schools and staff have high expectations of children's behaviour – given their age and understanding – we tend to get more positive outcomes. School policies should set out these expectations and highlight firm but slightly elastic boundaries. If we praise and reinforce the behaviours we would ideally like to see, try our best to ignore some of the ones we would really rather didn't happen, and concentrate on teaching skills, it generally makes for a happier environment. Positive systems work far better than punitive systems. We need to have realistic beliefs; we can only seek to influence children's behaviour; we can't actually change it ourselves. The reward for positive behaviour should be the fact that the children have a happier time, although positive whole-school reward systems and classroom rewards also work well. Adults should be constantly vigilant and notice all the children who are behaving in appropriate ways – catching them 'being good' and commenting with specific praise both verbally and non-verbally. Verbal praise can be used to develop a child's intrinsic motivation: 'Well done, Vivienne, you have completed that problem. I am sure you could do a harder one.' Sometimes, however, we may need to additionally reward certain children when they have learned the skills to behave in a way that comes more naturally to other children whose skill set is already more highly developed. In other words, one size does not fit all. Sticking rigidly to a reward system does not lead to a level playing field. In fact, tangible rewards for all children whatever their age, as a concrete way of telling them how pleased we are with them, are a good thing, although they do need to be linked to emotional feedback. As adults, we appreciate when somebody says thank you to us or maybe gives us a little something for our efforts. Children are no different. Rewards shouldn't be seen as bribes. They are simply a way of acknowledging something that has been done well or a new skill that has been learned. They are a way of building up confidence and developing appropriate self-esteem.

Positive behaviour needs to be taught. It is not somehow caught! Adults need to model it, both to children and among themselves. Adults can't really expect children to hold doors open for each other if they do not also hold doors open. If adults in a school don't say 'please' and 'thank you' when they speak to each other, children cannot be expected to do the same. When adults model helping behaviours, children watch, listen and have a chance to copy.

When modelling behaviours, it is sometimes useful for the adults to do this in a slightly exaggerated way.

Adults are showing children what to do. Sometimes children don't notice. As adults in a school, if we praise each other and do it in a noticeable but still genuine way, children do realise. If we do the same thing in a hushed whisper, nobody other than the adult to whom we are speaking is aware, so there is no opportunity provided for copying.

Model the behaviour that you wish to see, and try not to over-emphasise the behaviours that you don't. This may seem very obvious, but actually adults' behaviour is a highly significant influence. Act as a role model for children who are in the process of developing their own social skills and their ability to make choices. You don't have to be perfect – we all make mistakes – but if you do make one, apologise.

Children very quickly pick up on adults' behaviour: they watch, listen, absorb. Tone of voice is important as children tune in to this. They also very quickly pick up on who responds to them and in what ways, depending on what they are doing. Consider the language between adults in your classroom. Listen for a session and see what the adults are actually saying and how.

Think and reflect

Is there anything you need to change?

Do the adults in your classroom interact with each other enough?

Where staff consistently model the same positive approaches, children pick up on this more quickly, the general behaviour within the school and classroom becomes more positive, and everybody is happier. Consistency is really key – not because it is focussed on during inspections, but because children (and adults) need to feel secure and know where they stand. Inconsistent expectations confuse children, and staff as well! Obviously, at times we need to differentiate expectations and approaches because of individual needs – but, overall, practice needs to be positive and very consistent, so there is no room for confusion.

Where staff model positive behaviours and positive behaviour management to other staff, the approach becomes even more consistent. We all learn by watching and listening to others. If you have an approach that you find works, tell your colleagues and let them test it out for themselves. If you are struggling with something, ask other members of staff what they would do in your situation.

Be aware of your own body language: the way that you sit, stand, walk; the way you act as children enter the classroom at the start of each session. If you move purposefully, you present as being more confident. Body language communicates a high proportion of any message; subtleties such as raising your eyebrows, hand gestures and facial expressions all contribute. Folding your arms can be said to create a barrier; a more open posture invites people in. Children are learning to read body language as they learn to respond to spoken language. Think about yours.

Think and reflect

Watch the body language of other staff in different situations. Can you learn from it?

4

Focussing on Primary Behaviours and Least to Most Intrusive Interventions

A primary behaviour is the first behaviour that you would rather not see in a situation where you have to intervene. This may be very different from the final behaviour exhibited by the child. The tendency is to focus on the final behaviour, and I am suggesting that this is not always terribly helpful in trying to teach the skills needed in order to lessen the chances of the particular difficulty happening again.

An example might be Sue snatching a lovely sharpened pencil from Belinda. This is completely unprovoked: she just goes up to Belinda, who is working quietly, and whizzes it out of her hands. Belinda screams loudly and tries to get it back. Sue runs off around the classroom, throws the pencil on the floor, stamps on it and breaks it. The primary behaviour in this case is the snatching: the first incident. It is easy to get drawn in and focus on the issue of breaking the pencil, particularly as you know Belinda loves to sharpen her pencils and write with them. It is the same if a child ends up talking back to you. The talking-back is not the primary behaviour – don't get drawn in!

Focus on the primary behaviour – the snatching – because if the pencil hadn't been snatched in the first place, it wouldn't have been broken.

Some children are just beginning to learn about the consequences of their own actions for themselves and for others, but we can't assume these concepts are secure. Remember that social and emotional competencies develop at different rates. Some children may well not be able to put themselves in the other child's place. They are likely to require help in resolving conflict. Adults can help by trying to get each child to describe or show what happened and by making sure that they very obviously listen to both sides of the story when accounts differ. It is useful to reflect back what the child has said: 'So, Belinda, you are upset and cross because you were working quietly with your pencil and Sue took it.' 'You got angry/sad, Sue, because you wanted use that pencil/were a bit stuck with your work.' Sometimes children only have developing concepts of the meaning of the words 'happy' and 'sad' – it depends on the child – but be aware of this. Angry and sad may be the same thing to Sue. It's not just about Sue's vocabulary; it's about her understanding. This can confuse the issue. Depending on the children's understanding, it can be helpful to ask their opinion as to what should happen next, along with a rule reminder: 'Remember, Sue, we put our hands up and wait if we are having difficulties with our work, and then someone comes to help us.'

When adults do have to intervene because they see something that is inappropriate within the context, it is useful to do it in a 'least to most intrusive' way. This means – unless, of course, the situation is dangerous – that staff make the smallest intervention first.

Focussing attention on the children behaving appropriately – catching children 'being good' while ignoring the one who hasn't quite got round to it yet – can be a useful starting point: 'Oh, well done, Paolo and Chris; I can see that you have started your work already. Thank you' (while keeping an eye on Emma, sitting next to Paolo, who is still thinking about beginning hers). If Emma then realises that it is time to get on, make sure you say thank you to her as well.

A 'look' across the classroom is often enough, sometimes accompanied by a gesture. There is no need to say anything as this disrupts the flow of the lesson. It's the silent 'I have seen what you are doing/not doing – now make the right choice'!

Using your own physical proximity is another useful, least-intrusive strategy. You don't have to say anything. Sometimes moving towards the child who is doing the thing you would rather they did not do will work in prompting them to behave in a more positive way. If you go just about close enough to nearly invade their personal space so they definitely notice you are there, but not so close that your actions can cause anxiety, often the child's behaviour will change. Again, make a positive comment when it does. This also works with adults if you ever have to lead a staff meeting!

Using simple questions to refocus: gently approach the child and ask them a simple question not related to the behaviour you would rather not see: 'That looks good, Laura. Are you using the blue paint or the red paint?' (She is busy tipping the blue paint out all over the floor.) 'Yes, that's right: blue. Go and find me some blue bricks out of that box while I just tidy up this paint so people don't slip in it.'

Give a clear rule reminder: 'Keith, remember our walking rule.' He stops running. 'Good boy, that's excellent walking.' Remember to say exactly which behaviour is good; make your praise specific. 'Good boy' by itself is not as effective. 'Keith, do not run' is not very effective at all in terms of teaching the rule, because if Keith wanted to be awkward, he could decide to slither along the corridor like a snake instead. Say what you want to see!

The tone of your voice is important here. If you adapt your voice levels and tone appropriately to match your message, there is a greater chance of the message getting through. Mood can be altered relatively easily by altering the tone of your voice.

Your own presence in various areas of the classroom helps immensely with general management. Yes, you may need to work with a group, but you don't have to sit constantly with that group; you have a responsibility for the learning of all members of the class. Likewise, you don't have to stay at the front, glued to your whiteboard. One of the best pre-emptive strategies is to move around, making positive comments when you do, helping children to remain on task but also noticing anyone having difficulties. Use eye scanning as you do this. Be aware of what is happening in every area of your classroom – just imagine you are an insect with compound eyes!

5

Rights, Rules and Relationships

Within any school everyone has rights – children and adults. These four basic rights underpin your behaviour policy:

1 Children's right to learn.

2 Your right to teach/develop/instruct.

3 Everybody's right to safety.

4 Everybody's right to dignity and respect.

These allow you and your children to feel safe. The framework of your behaviour policy enables you to make decisions about your response to children's behaviour. It enables you to go beyond 'Do it because I told you to' and should lead to some consistency across the school. A behaviour policy should not be a 'discipline' policy. It isn't about punishment; it's about how the school policy is going to enable positive behaviour to be taught and celebrated.

Schools have rules. A few simple ones are best – ones that work equally well in the outdoor environment as in the indoor one. Rules should sit within the behaviour policy of the establishment which should conform to any current government guidance. Rules should be phrased positively: for example, 'We speak nicely to each other' rather than 'Do not shout'; 'We walk inside' rather than 'Do not run.' Rules should describe the behaviour we wish to see. Rules should be displayed pictorially and in simple text in all areas of the school. Even up to Year 6, rules need pictures! As with other displays, they should be put in a prominent place. They should be relatively large, to enable you to use them as a teaching aid. Something A4-size stuck on the back of your classroom door is neither appropriate nor helpful.

Very often you will find a set of whole-school rules within the school's behaviour policy. These are usually displayed around the school, in shared areas and corridors, and also outside on the playground.

Many classrooms often have a set of these rules displayed too. Where things can get confusing is when classrooms also have their own rules. I would suggest that there is no need to have two sets! I agree that, depending on the ages of the children in the class, school rules may need to be unpicked and phrased differently in order that children really understand what they mean. Rules such as 'We behave appropriately' need discussion and might end up as 'We are kind' in some younger classes. However, having two different sets of rules just confuses everyone and leads to a lack of continuity throughout the school. If children receive rewards for keeping the rules in one class and then move to another class where the rules are different, there is no consistency in rewarding positive behaviour in the school as a whole and so the point of having whole-school rules on which to build rewards is lost.

There is, of course, some mileage in working with the children in your class with a view to them taking ownership of the way the school rules are interpreted. In other words, you are not aiming to get them to create a whole set of new rules but asking them to explore their understanding and maybe rephrase the ones used across the school.

Rules need to be actively taught, spoken about, acted out, painted, used in role play, etc. in appropriate ways depending on the age and understanding of the children. One assembly by the headteacher at the beginning of the year is not adequate or useful. Your rules will require a level of understanding in order to be followed. Children need to be taught the necessary skills in a very practical and concrete way over and over again throughout the year. Rules, and also routines (for example, putting equipment away, taking off boots when coming inside, hanging coats, giving out equipment, lining up) all need to be taught and revisited frequently. This is not something for the beginnings of terms; it is something that is ongoing. Predictable regular routines – with sometimes slightly elastic boundaries and warnings of transitions – are important in making sure children feel secure. Reviewing your routines is a useful thing to do: think about why you have them and the skills that they teach.

Think and reflect

Are your routines fit for purpose?

If you have your own classroom rules, are they sufficiently aligned to the school rules?

How would a stranger coming into your classroom know what the rules were?

Do you give warnings of transitions?

Rules need to be reinforced constantly and in the most concrete and practical way. For younger children, for example, if a new toy or puppet is introduced to the class, it can help if the children explain the rules to it to make sure it gets on well with everybody. Large glove puppets are excellent for this, and if they can be made to behave inappropriately, children will delight in telling them what they should do instead. Older children may wish to write a letter to an alien describing the rules of their class should they want to come and visit. It doesn't really matter which vehicle you use to teach your rules, only that you do actively teach them.

The purpose of the rules is so that staff can refer to them when they see children keeping them. Rules are definitely not there in order for staff (and other children) to catch children when they break them. Some staff seem to have difficulties with this (hangers and floggers!) and it is about changing a mindset in order to look for positives and give rewards. Some children may like to focus on other children when they are not following the rules. Catch all children being 'good' and particularly catch children who find this difficult at times. Catch them keeping the rules and give immediate positive feedback if you can; if this is not possible, make sure that you tell the child at a later stage in the session that you saw them doing whatever they did and that you are so pleased with them. This works so much better than telling children off when they inadvertently – or sometimes deliberately – fail to follow the rules. If you notice and praise the behaviours that you want to see, you will get more of them. Confrontational styles can produce adverse reactions. Having rules to refer to scaffolds staff responses. This is why it is helpful to have your rules displayed prominently in your classroom: it reminds you to look for children keeping them, and then every time you refer to them and point towards them while praising a child, all the other children get a little rule reminder too. Actively looking for children keeping the rules makes such a difference to the tone of a class. If you have a child who focusses on rules being broken by others, ask them to start spotting positives for you too. Test it out. Catch the children in your class following one of your rules and comment positively and specifically when you notice. Have a look at the impact on the child concerned, on the children near them and on you and other staff. What do you notice?

Although it may seem overly simplistic, just by concentrating on using positive language, and by using it frequently, adults can have an impact on children's behaviour. Describe the behaviours you want to see.

We all tend to function more happily within the context of positive relationships. Babies form relationships with their primary caregiver from the moment they are born and develop a bond. Small children form relationships with their family and friends and extend these relationships when they meet new children and adults in their early years setting. Relationships change and develop throughout a child's years in primary education.

Relationships that value others will raise self-esteem and help them to grow.

Relationships in schools between children and children, between children and adults and between adults and adults are all important to consider. When relationships between adults are supportive and positive, a whole lot more is achieved. We build relationships over time with children and adults when we do fairly simple things: when we greet people by name; when we stop and have a little chat; when we make eye contact and give them our full attention, even if it is only for a minute; and when we remind both children and adults of something they have done well. We should treat children with the same degree of respect as we believe we ourselves are due. Even when we need to correct them or remind them of a rule, we need to maintain their dignity and protect their self-esteem. Sometimes we have to build relationships consciously with children because by getting to know them better we can sometimes gain an insight into some of the behaviours we see.

6

Observing Behaviour Within a Classroom

It is as important to observe positive behaviour as it is to observe the behaviours that you would rather did not occur. When we mention 'observing behaviour', the first thing that tends to spring to mind is that we are going to observe and look for the problems. This tends to be the trigger for observation; however, it is as important to look for a child's strengths and interests, in order to be able to build on them, as it is to look for the things they may be doing 'wrong'. Observation by adults builds empathy and aids planning. Stepping back and observing the things that are going well is time very well spent, and none of us do this often enough.

The very word 'behaviour' is subjective. Therefore, it is important to get as unbiased a view as possible. Unwanted behaviour in children generally causes emotional reactions in adults. However, adults' reactions are different depending on their own world view. Some adults find swearing very offensive, particularly when children are involved; for other adults, maybe spitting pushes their buttons. It is important to be aware of what pushes your own buttons – the things you dislike most – because you may be more liable to react to these sorts of behaviours than others.

Any persistent unwanted behaviours are wearing. It doesn't matter how 'serious' or 'trivial' these behaviours are; it's the frequency and persistency that is significant. Staff get worn down and almost anticipate the next incident. This again affects staff behaviour, and sometimes it can become a self-fulfilling prophecy. Every time Jeremy lines up, you are waiting for him to poke the child in front of him in the back; every time Monty plays football there seems to be an 'incident'.

If you have concerns about a particular child, the use of a basic checklist can be a good starting point. This should be a positive checklist. Look at the things the child can do. Can they repeat instructions? follow a one- or two-part verbal instruction? collect equipment for a task? stay on task for two, five, ten minutes? value completed work, construction etc.? follow routines? gain the attention of adults appropriately? take turns? sit appropriately for a short length of time? share equipment? respond to praise? take responsibility for a job? tidy up when asked? keep their hands and feet to themselves? make positive comments to peers? initiate and maintain friendships? use appropriate table manners? Focus on what they are able to do in the broadest sense rather than anything that might be causing them a bit of a problem. This gives you a baseline at a particular point in time within a particular context. Your checklist should then point you towards areas that need a bit of work and the skills you need to teach. Think of the situations available to you to teach maybe two of the skills that need to be developed. Plan and monitor. Don't forget to date the checklist and revisit it in about six weeks so you can tell if your teaching is having an impact.

Your basic checklist should have given you an indication as to which sorts of behaviours/skills may be of concern and would potentially need support to develop; this might help you with further targeted observations should you feel they are needed.

When observing, note only the behaviours you actually see in clear terms – for example, not 'Trish was naughty' but 'Trish was out of seat.' Quite often reports of misdemeanours contain non-specific language. If another member of staff tells you that Emily's behaviour in assembly was 'appalling', ask them to describe it to you in terms of what they actually saw; 'appalling' is a subjective word. When observing, make sure you include all behaviours, exactly as you see them. Don't discount any because you feel you can 'explain' why the child behaves in this way; if you do discount some, you will only get a partial picture. Maybe observe for three-quarters of an hour and tally positive and negative behaviours. Look at interactions, both adult- and child-initiated. Look at facial expressions and body language. Make a note of context, time of day, temperature and noise level. As well as observing the child themselves, you are observing the room as a whole, but in a more general way. In addition to noting frequency of behaviours, look for persistency and severity. Then, ideally, come back and look at the same child again another time. Compare your findings.

Again, you are looking to create a baseline – something that is as objective as possible – in order to see which skills you need to develop next. If you don't feel you can be impartial (there is nothing wrong with this), consider asking somebody else within the context to observe for you, or do a paired observation. This forms part of the school's *assess, plan, do, review* cycle, and at a later stage can be fed into the school's special education and disabilities structure if there is a need. In many cases, assessing, planning, doing and reviewing at an earlier stage can be sufficient, but at times when it isn't, records of progress, changes to classroom strategies and also interventions can be useful in building up a picture and acting as a record that is invaluable should the child's needs escalate.

Don't forget to observe the reactions the child receives from both staff and other children. Remember that all behaviour has a reason and that one person's behaviour has an impact on another's.

Think and reflect

Do you understand your school's assess, plan, do, review *cycle?*

Do the observation forms/checklists you use actually make sense to you, and do they help you to move forward practically?

When you have identified a basic skill that you think would make a difference, set out how you are going to teach it. You might have identified several skills, but choose one or maybe two priorities. Concerns that potentially endanger the safety of the child, other children and staff will need to come high on the list.

Think and reflect

What situations are you going to create for the child to learn and practise this skill?

You will have to teach the new skill many times – how are you going to know when it has been learned?

How exactly are you going to teach it?

Maybe look at this same skill in about six weeks after you have actively tried to teach it in the way in which you decided. Initially, you will need to use the resources available to you within the classroom in terms of adult support. This may well need some changes. Maybe at a later date, support for this child will come from within the resources of the school's special educational needs and disabilities system.

Discussing your ideas with colleagues is essential, as you all need to understand which skills you are trying to develop in order to have a consistent approach concerning a particular child.

However, when talking about this, don't forget to mind your language as you describe behaviour! 'Cheeky' means different things to different people. Describe the behaviour you see: 'Emma told Mrs Albion she had dropped her dinner down her front while she was eating her lunch and it was still all over her blouse.' This tells you exactly what Emma did. It is so much better than 'Emma was cheeky to Mrs Albion.' Your colleague tells you: 'Laura has been very rude on the playground this morning.' You need to find out exactly what she did here because 'rude' is a very woolly term! When filling in observation forms and checklists with colleagues, you really do need to get down to specifics in terms of what you have seen and experienced through working with the child, and try to avoid ambiguous language.

7

Antecedents, Behaviour and Consequences

Sometimes, for a one-off incident, staff find that looking at the situation in terms of antecedents, behaviour and consequences (ABC) is helpful. The antecedents are what was happening immediately before – for example, before one child slapped another in the face. If you are using an ABC form, start in the middle. Start with the behaviour of the child, then note the behaviour of the staff and the other children around. Then look at the antecedents – again, for the child and for everyone else. Finally, look at the consequences in the same way. In fact, think of it as BAC!

Make it broader than the incident itself. Focussing your attention on what happened before (the antecedents) and what the outcome was (the consequences) can often be far more effective than focussing energy on the event itself.

Think and reflect

Are there any noticeable antecedents for the victim?

Has this child ever been a victim before?

What were the antecedents for staff? Who was nearest? What were they doing?

Then for the behaviour itself – given the behaviour that you actually saw – what happened?

Again, for all three (the aggressor, victim and staff): what did they do? And what were the immediate consequences for all three?

At times this is helpful in trying to make sense of a situation. It may be worth repeating if the same child is involved in further incidents. Sometimes a pattern begins to emerge. And sometimes not, but at least in considering the situation in this way you stand to gain some small insights and can better plan for the future. The information you gain from the exercise is of no use if you don't do anything with it. Sometimes a small change can make all the difference.

Often there may be no need to use overly complicated methods to improve a child's behavioural skills.

When you have identified an area for development, it may mean that by changing the antecedents you can affect the undesired behaviour. For example, you can pre-empt the situation, make sure you have communicated clear expectations or give an early warning. You can change the background/context in which the behaviour occurs, remove temptation, change the setting or, for some children, perhaps introduce an agreed prompt. This is not avoiding the issue; it is attempting to create success.

If there is a consequence to a child's behaviour, it is important the child understands that it is the behaviour you don't like and that can't happen here, but you still like them as a person. Separate the behaviour from the person. It is important to keep relationships intact and focus on how to move on. Always protect the child's self-esteem.

It is also important to give children take-up time when you give them an instruction. Often children can get so engrossed in what they are doing that they do not even notice what is going on around them. Using their name before an instruction can be helpful – with a little pause to let it sink in that you are talking to them: 'Julian (pause), Julian...it is tidy-up time now.' If you say thank you after an instruction, it gives the impression that you expect compliance: 'Marcel (pause)...Marcel, put the books back on the shelf; thanks' or 'Flo (pause)... Flo, switch the computer off now; thanks.'

8

Rewards and Sanctions

A school/class reward system, along with the relationships built between children and staff, have to provide an incentive for positive behaviour, ideally to such an extent that sanctions are very rarely needed. Rewards should be applied across the whole school, including during breaks and lunchtimes.

It can be useful to begin by looking at the sorts of behaviours you want to see and encourage around school. These might include speaking to staff and peers with respect, using appropriate voice levels, putting a hand up in class when appropriate, showing respect for property, keeping equipment tidy, listening to others' point of view, being kind to others, walking inside the building, following instructions and many more.

Once you have thought about what it is that you actually want in a very practical way, it is also useful to consider how you currently actively teach the skills needed for these positive behaviours. These sorts of behaviours, which will be covered in more global terms within your school rules, are the ones you need to reward. There are many, many things that can be given as a reward – verbal praise, thumbs up, stickers, team points, letters home, recognition in assembly, going into lunch first, an extra five minutes on the computer – and each school has its own systems. It works better if there is as high a degree of consistency across classes as possible and if systems are not overly complicated. We have to get away from 'Why should I reward children for the things I just expect them to do?' and realise the value of rewarding 'ordinary' positive behaviour.

You may decide to target one behaviour for a few days across the school, rewarding pupils caught keeping the school rule that this behaviour most closely relates to. In class, it can be useful to set a behaviour objective for a particular lesson, letting the children know exactly what you will be looking for and giving rewards out when you see it.

Praise and reward should far outweigh sanctions. The power of positive praise and reward should not be underestimated!

Sanctions come a poor second to rewards, but it is acknowledged that they do have to be there. The plan should be to use them less and less.

It is useful to look at undesirable behaviours in three groups:

1   behaviour that is low level and is part of general classroom management skills

2   behaviour that requires a consequence from the class teacher because of its intensity or its frequency

3   behaviour that involves the involvement of
     senior staff.

Behaviours that might be in the first category are being out of seat, tapping a pen on the table, rocking back and forth on a chair, no homework, lying, name calling, snatching equipment, stopping other children from working, and pushing in the line. These all require management from the class teacher: a look, a gesture, moving closer, a rule reminder, a warning or a small sanction such as missing five minutes of break time.

Behaviours in the second category might include persistent arguing and talking back, fighting, stealing, bullying and verbal abuse towards staff and children. These still need management by the class teacher. If class teachers are not seen to sanction more serious behaviours, it can lead to a loss of respect and a feeling that the teacher can't or won't do anything, and therefore the behaviours can escalate. Sanctions might involve losing complete break times, a warning/sad note home to the child's parents or carers, or maybe a phone call to parents from the class teacher. If these behaviours persist and increase in intensity and frequency, it may be that the class teacher tells the child that he or she will be speaking to a member of the senior management. The child still needs to see the class teacher as being in charge.

Behaviours in the third category might include racial or homophobic abuse, persistent bullying, physical abuse towards staff and dangerous refusal to follow instructions. Each school will have its own list of actions for which children need to be referred to the headteacher. These should be few in number; otherwise the impact of sanctions by the head can be lost. Referral to the headteacher for positive reasons should be far more frequent!

Remember, sanctions do not need to be immediate. It's often the certainty rather than the severity which makes the difference!

Rewards and sanctions may need to be differentiated for children with additional needs. It is perfectly fine to do this in the same way in which you differentiate maths and reading books. This is why behaviour policies have to have elastic boundaries. By differentiating, you are actually creating a level playing field and making the reasonable adjustments necessary to support the child to succeed. The fear that anarachy will be caused if class teachers give more rewards to one child or slightly differentiate their expectations is unfounded! Remember: if your behaviour policy states that you will make reasonable adjustments (which it should), you do not have to discuss your use of rewards and sanctions with any parent other than the parent of the child in question. You wouldn't dream of discussing the number of stickers in another child's science book with a parent who felt their child should have had more, and this is exactly the same thing.

A final word on rewards and sanctions. Many schools publish lists of inappropriate behaviours with the relevant sanction next to them. If you are going to do this, make sure it's a list or a 'positive behaviour ladder' that first of all spells out positive behaviours and their rewards, as well as negative ones and their sanctions. Start with the positives right at the top. Emphasise the rewards. Give the negatives far less importance. The focus of your systems should be on encouraging the sorts of behaviours that you want to see rather than on the punitive aspects!

Think and reflect

How do your rewards tie in with your school rules?

Do you focus on catching children being 'good'?

Why do you send children to the headteacher?

9

How Do Schools Teach Self-Regulation?

Both academic learning and behavioural learning require well-developed skills of self-regulation. Schools already do this. This is about enabling children to recognise their emotions and organise their experiences in such a way that their needs are met. In the end, children need to be able to choose for themselves to behave in certain ways in certain situations. They need to be able to evaluate a situation using their senses and previous experiences and respond in the way that they feel is best. It doesn't need a separate curriculum, it isn't an isolated skill; it is something that can be developed through everyday experiences. It involves the ability to regulate both positive and negative emotions, the things we enjoy and make us happy, as well as the things that upset us or make us angry or sad.

Among the skills and attributes needed to develop this are self-awareness; self-confidence and appropriate self-esteem; understanding and expressing your own feelings and developing an understanding of the feelings of others; appreciating that there are choices; the ability to make decisions; and the ability to communicate effectively.

Teaching problem-solving skills is a big step towards independence. In everyday matters, such as putting on your own PE kit, moving from one area of the school to another and finding your way back, or working out how equipment fits together, staff can scaffold the learning.

Making choices about, for example, the equipment necessary for a task, whose partner to be or what to have for lunch supports children in learning to evaluate their likes and dislikes and teaches sharing and turn-taking skills, while helping to develop self-control. For younger children, pouring out their own drink from a jug and even serving drinks to others promotes independence, the ability to make choices, self-confidence and social skills.

The use of set routines at the end of sessions teaches children to work together and to tidy away their belongings. This encourages respect for others and for the things in their environment.

Learning a new skill, such as collage or a ball skill, may help a child to further understand their own strengths and weaknesses. Taking turns in a game encourages the development of attention skills and the skill of waiting. Building towers with blocks so high that they eventually fall over, and then starting again, encourages persistence when faced with difficult problems.

When adults talk about their own emotions, it can help children to access strategies to help them manage their feelings. For example, 'I am feeling unhappy today because my daughter has gone back to university – but I am going to have a chat to her on the phone when I get home and I will see her in three weeks.'

None of these are things that do not already happen regularly within the school environment. For some children, there may be a need to structure in some of these types of activities more regularly in order to increase their skills and understanding of themselves.

Giving children responsibilities, no matter how small, is likely to lead that child to behave in a more careful manner towards other people and belongings. The impact is not always immediate, as it is a skill to be learned, but it is one well worth teaching!

Thinking about how self-regulation develops leads adults to become more aware of their own emotions and their own ability to self-regulate. This in turn enables them to reflect on children's individual needs. Adults are then able to model, prompt, hint and cue the child in, so the child then learns for him- or herself.

10

The Importance of Environments and Their Impact on Behaviour

The quality of a child's learning environment is extremely important – both the indoor and the outdoor environment. It goes without saying that you teach in the classroom you are given, with the number of children that you have in your class, and that some things may be difficult or impossible to change. However, there are elements that you can work on which will have an impact on the children's well-being and learning. Given that all behaviour happens within a context, it is possible to teach social, emotional and behavioural skills by modifying the environment. The actual quality of the school and classroom environment is paramount – both the physical one and the emotional environment created by well-trained and sympathetic staff who strive to develop children's own skills.

An overwhelmingly noisy environment is likely to lead to a prevalence of shouting in order to be heard. A silent one can stifle conversation, cooperation and language development. It's about getting a balance and, again, about expectations. Actively teaching voice levels and practising them in appropriate contexts helps. Playground voice, partner voice and silence are really all that is needed. Practise playground voice outside, not inside – it's a louder outside voice not to be used in the classroom! Children will respond well to a reminder of the voice levels to be used at the beginning of each session, and over time it will become part of their routine.

Predictable classroom routines help to build security and self-confidence in all children and are of particular use for children who are still developing their social skills. Equipment that is clearly labelled, kept in regular places and always tidied up before children leave the classroom; a space to put their own things and their own label on their tray; always entering and leaving the room in a calm and controlled way – all these things help to build security.

We can scaffold learning by the areas and the equipment we offer. A couple of comfortable chairs in a book corner lends itself to sharing a book. A tidy bookcase helps children to put books back tidily.

Sharing and turn-taking skills can be developed if we consider the equipment we make available for any given activity: for example, a maths activity with shared equipment in the centre of the table, but not quite enough for everyone; or a cooking activity, making pizza slices in a group of four with only one pizza cutter. Football outside at playtime can be for one class one day and another class the next. Board games are also excellent for this, but most day-to-day activities that you have planned for your class can be modified slightly in order to encourage sharing, turn-taking and the development of social skills. Sometimes it is the simplest things that encourage children to develop the skills they need.

Look at your indoor flooring. As well as being clean, is it fit for purpose? Does it perhaps demark areas? Is your carpet space big enough for all the children to sit on without being squashed? Do you have regular carpet places so everyone knows where they sit and who will be sitting around them? Does the layout of your tables ensure you can walk between them when you are moving around the room?

Children who have difficulty concentrating should be seated in areas of low traffic, where other children pass infrequently, rather than in areas that many children pass in order to get equipment or to reach their own seats. Some children may be better staying in their own seat while working with different groups, with the remainder of the group moving to their table. When considering the layout of your tables, it may be useful to also consider placing them in a horseshoe or double horseshoe – where it is still perfectly possible for children to work with partners or in small groups. In whichever way you decide to lay out your tables, consider social and emotional need as well as academic needs.

Respect for equipment in any environment is a skill that may need to be taught to some children. This should be covered by your classroom rules, and praise for the correct use of equipment is a good motivator. Misuse of equipment is often something that causes problems. While we want to teach Paolo to be independent in his use of scissors, and so we leave them in a pot on the centre of his table, he doesn't seem to be able to stop stabbing his neighbours with them. There is nothing wrong with removing the pot. Often pre-empting incidents can be the best strategy! Paolo will eventually learn to use the scissors, but perhaps now is not the best time.

Think and reflect

Review your environment often. Is it stimulating and fit for purpose?

Would it be interesting to you if you were a child?

Would you be motivated to learn here?

Are the noise levels in your classroom appropriate?

Is your seating plan working?

11

What We Mean by Nurture

To me, nurture means looking after, caring for, helping to grow. We nurture all sorts of things: we nurture plants (helping them to grow strongly) and we nurture our own interests (developing them, honing them, becoming more proficient and knowledgeable). Those of us lucky enough to be parents nurture our children to the best of our abilities, to help them to grow up into strong, healthy, caring human beings who can stand on their own two feet. This means meeting emotional needs as well as physical needs.

In schools we try to offer a safe base where children can flourish. Children need the unconditional love of a parent or caregiver and approval from those who are important to them. Staff in school are very important to the children who attend. Children respond best to clear signals, so it is important that approval is made explicit. They also need security and for both their physical needs and emotional needs to be met. It is important to see each child as an individual and help them to develop their skills from their own unique starting point. It is also important to have a non-judgemental attitude and maybe to move away from 'normal' expectations of behaviour at any given age.

When adults listen – really listen – and then respond to children, share activities and take an interest, bonds are formed. When adults praise even the smallest of things, children respond and their self-esteem grows; through this, the child's understanding of themselves and the world around them grows, they begin to develop empathy and sympathy, and they blossom.

Children all see the world differently as a result of their life experiences to date. For the vast majority of children, you will have little or no knowledge of their prior experiences, and for the vast majority of children there is no need to have any. The quality of early relationships is overwhelmingly important. Sometimes children have had difficult early relationships. By nurturing these children in particular, we can help build pathways to aid in their understanding of their world. Sometimes the experiences we give may need to be very similar to those we would give to a much younger child. Emotional age is not always the same as chronological age. This is an important factor, but early childhood/baby experiences given in an age-appropriate way can sometimes help to shape the children we see at four, five, six years – and older. It is all about looking to develop a child's skills from the place that they are at – and every child in your class will be in a slightly different place.

Language is a way to express feelings. Sometimes, without the appropriate vocabulary to express themselves, children 'act out' their feelings. All children can benefit from developing their feelings vocabulary. Using words instead of actions is another skill to be taught. Informally as well as formally, the language of emotion is a great help in enabling communication and progressing social and emotional development. If you don't have a reasonable understanding of what 'happy' is, and what 'sad' is, how do you know how to make another person happy? If you don't know the difference between the words 'angry' and 'scared', and can't express yourself, maybe you are more likely to hit out in frustration.

Think of your own facial expressions. You can communicate a myriad of emotions without words. Children need to learn to pick up on these visual cues. Some children manage to do this more easily than others. Having a mirror near the door of the classroom and encouraging children to use it to make faces, show emotions and develop the associated language can be hugely successful, but it takes time. Then, as children's vocabulary develops more and more, words can be added, until by Year 6 the majority of your class may be able to both make and recognise a discombobulated face!

Think and reflect

Do you actively teach the language of emotion?

Do you start from where a child is at and nurture them?

12

Whole-School Approaches

Whole-school approaches have a focus on prevention of need, and early intervention when a need arises. Early intervention itself is not enough; although it is useful to meet a need as soon as possible, intervening only once a need is apparent is a bit like closing the stable door once the horse has bolted.

Resources spent on whole-school prevention strategies are invaluable as they affect all children and staff and then have a knock-on effect in terms of the number of strategies needed for individual children. Having an excellent and effective whole-school behaviour policy, based on positives, praise and reward, is an invaluable preventative strategy and is all too often overlooked!

Teaching a whole-school social and emotional curriculum designed to develop the skills of all children in all classes really makes a difference. This can then be built upon should individual children need a little more of the same. This is time very well spent.

Yoga, mindfulness and peer massage as part of the curriculum are preventative; all have an impact and do not single anyone out. Worries about 'lost' curriculum time should be set aside. The benefits in terms of mental health and well-being, social skills and cohesion, which in turn affect children's general functioning – including their academic learning – far outweigh any negatives. These things only take a matter of minutes and can be done regularly.

Nurture groups, when run well, are a whole-school early intervention strategy.

It is important that whole-school preventative strategies include everyone. If we take a definition of inclusion to be 'the feeling derived from being included', we also have to be aware that there is a feeling derived from being excluded!

Think and reflect

Are you inclusive?

13

Additional Needs

Some children in school require additional support in developing their social and emotional skills. Some but not necessarily all of these children will fall within the remit of the Special Educational Needs and Disabilities Code of Practice, and will need skills teaching and developing in more specific ways than the majority of their peers. The vast majority of these children will not have an Education, Health and Care Plan. For most, this simply isn't necessary if appropriate and planned support can be given by skilled staff in school, and classroom management and whole-school policies are supportive. Many of these children will not have a diagnosis of a particular need; where they do, there may be co-morbid needs that also need to be met. A diagnosis itself does not lead to additional support. Researching needs and then honing strategies and interventions refine the approach taken and increase the likelihood of support being successful. An understanding of the types of strategies that have helped particular 'types' of children who at times display 'acting out' or withdrawn behaviours can be useful. I cannot stress enough, however, that every child needs to be treated as an individual, and support tailored to meet their needs is likely to be the most effective.

With this in mind, I offer some *basic* strategies grouped into areas of need. These are intended as a starting point, as obviously I don't know the details of the child you may be thinking about as you are reading this!

All of these strategies work best within positive whole-school policies and good classroom systems.

1. Strategies helpful for children with social communication needs or ASD

- Give clear instructions; rephrase if necessary.

- Realise that whole-class instructions may not be noticed – the child may not realise they apply to them. Use their name and allow take-up time before giving an instruction.

- Try to be unambiguous, avoid humour and irony, and check understanding.

- Have clear rules and use them positively. Reinforce them regularly and make your expectations clear.

- Minimise disruption of routines. Warn of forthcoming disruptions and rehearse if appropriate. Try to keep to your daily routine as far as possible; if there is a last-minute change, explain this to the child.

- Be aware of literalities. Many difficulties have been caused when staff felt a child was being rude, but actually they were merely following instructions to the letter. Think about what you are saying. Try to avoid idioms and unspoken assumptions.

- Don't get offended when the child makes a literal comment: 'Miss, your hair is a mess today' may be perfectly true!

- Provide a personal timetable. This may take the form of a task board or a little book to be kept in the child's pocket.

- Try to structure your classroom environment with the child in mind. If the child finds a personal workstation helpful, provide one.

- Focus on the things that a child can do rather than things that they find difficult. For example, if there is a difficulty with empathy, avoid 'Why do you think they did that?' or 'How do you think the others feel?' unless this is part of a structured programme.

- Realise that interests and obsessions can be intrinsically rewarding to the child, who may genuinely find it very hard to stop a particular activity. Try if possible to structure these in when planning.

- Know that generalisation may not occur. Just because a child can multiply three-digit numbers doesn't mean that they can complete simple multiplication word problems.

- Don't necessarily expect skills to transfer from one subject to another. Measurement learned for maths may have to be relearned for geography.

- Understand that the child may have significant difficulties interpreting the behaviour of others, including yours. The significance of 'the look' across the classroom may be lost!

- Look out for difficulties with motor control which may lead to avoidance of writing tasks and many losses of PE kit.

- Explicitly teach social skills.

- Make it clear what positive behaviours are. Make your praise specific.

- Recognise that changes in behaviour may be caused by anxiety or stress – don't take anything personally.

- State clearly what 'finished' means. Once the child has finished one of a particular type of calculation, they may feel no need to do the rest of the calculations on the sheet as they know they can do the task now.

2. Strategies helpful for children with attention needs, attention deficit disorder (ADD) or attention deficit hyperactivity disorder (ADHD)

- Have a very predictable routine and provide Velcro timetables, pocket timetables and prompt cards as appropriate.

- Seat the child close to the place you teach the whole class from, with their back to the rest of the class to minimise distractions.

- Try to surround the child with good role models whom they like.

- Make a workstation available in an area of reduced stimuli if the child finds it helpful.

- Give clear and concise directions and instructions. Write these down so the child doesn't have to keep them in their head.

- Ask for instructions to be repeated back to you to ensure there is an understanding before the task starts.

- Give tasks one at a time rather than in a list. You may need to break down some tasks. Don't be afraid to modify tasks spontaneously if needed.

- If you are assessing a child's skill level, make sure it is the skill you are assessing rather than their attention span.

- Use errands ('Go to Mr Williams and get…') to give short breaks.

- Do your best to avoid using the child's name constantly in front of the class to encourage them back on task. Develop a covert signal instead.

- Use tactical ignoring for low-level behaviours. Focus on the positives and give plenty of specific praise.

- Within elastic boundaries, don't be afraid to challenge negative behaviours, keep options open and give the child a get-out: 'If you can do this, then this will happen. If you choose to do that, then that will happen.'

- Discuss negative behaviours without an audience.

- Actively encourage the development of self-esteem and tolerance within the class as a whole.

3. Strategies helpful for children with oppositional defiant disorder

- Make your expectations clear and reward when expectations are met.

- Remind the child of what they are working towards and try to encourage them to keep on track.

- Ensure you warn of transitions – use a visual timetable/sand timer if it helps.

- Use empathetic statements which help the child to know that you understand how they feel: 'I know you are enjoying this art and don't want to leave it, but it is break time in five minutes so you will have to put it away. You will have time to do some more tomorrow.'

- Give direct instructions to reduce ambiguity and redirect if possible. Give a clear instruction as to what you want the child to do.

- Make your praise specific.

- Give choices wherever possible: 'Which of these two activities are you going to start with?'

- Have clear routines and structures, and try not to deviate from them where possible.

- Also see the strategies above for children with attention needs; some of them may be useful.

4. Strategies helpful for children with pathological demand avoidance

- Allow take-up time.

- Use indirect language: 'Let's see if we can…'

- Utilise the child's interests.

- Give choices or present the same activity in more than one way.

71

- Use humour.

- Use distraction.

- Be flexible in your approach.

- Use visual timetables.

- Depersonalise 'demands' by using a puppet or a toy.

- Use sand timers at points of transition.

- Use a feelings board and emotion cards if these help.

- Ensure the child has an exit strategy.

- Also see the strategies above for children with ASD; many, but not all, may be applicable.

5. Strategies which may be helpful for children with sensory processing disorder

- Seat away from distracting sources of noise, in an area of low traffic.

- Build in breaks.

- Allow physical activity.

- Use noise-cancelling earphones to reduce stimulation – for example, in assembly.

- Seat on an appropriate chair and encourage the child to put their feet flat on the floor and rest their elbows on the table.

- Be aware that changes in routine may be difficult.

- Actively teach turn-taking and social skills.

- Practise the appropriate language to be used in social situations.

- Also consider some of the strategies suggested above for children with attention needs.

6. Strategies for children with social, emotional and mental health needs

- Be aware that the behaviours you see are quite often the tip of the iceberg and that children need your support.

- Ensure your school and classroom systems are clear and fair.

- Realise that these children may well need flexible teaching arrangements.

- Actively teach and encourage positive interaction with peers and adults.

- Take a 'least to most intrusive' approach with regard to management.

- Specifically teach rules and routines.

- Give many, many more rewards than sanctions.

- Provide a safe and supportive environment.

- Use the strategies above for ASD and ADHD as appropriate.

- Build relationships.

- Anticipate incidents and avoid them. Don't persist in putting the child in situations where they are likely to fail.

- Be aware that, in supporting these children, you may need to change your own behaviour and challenge your own beliefs.

- Encourage peer support and help to build friendship groups. Be aware that these children can often become isolated.

- Don't forget to assess for underlying learning needs.

14

The Special Educational Needs Code of Practice and Children with Behavioural Needs

The *assess, plan, do, review* cycle for any particular child may lead the class teacher to approach the schools special educational needs and disabilities coordinator (SENDCO) for advice. The responsibility for differentiation, planning and monitoring of any strategies and interventions lies with the class teacher, but SENDCOs are there to offer support and advice.

Once classroom-level strategies and basic interventions have been evaluated, it may be felt that a more targeted approach still needs to be taken and an individual plan may be written for the child. SENDCOs can give advice on appropriate, achievable target-setting and ways to monitor. There may be human resources that can be directed towards the child for the duration of the plan, or it may be that any existing classroom resource is directed away from other children for a short time to implement more specific interventions. If there is a behavioural concern, I would recommend that the plan is reviewed at least every six weeks – no longer. The 'targets' on the plan have to be measurable and achievable. You should be looking for very small steps that, with support, can be taught over a six-week period. The targets should be steps in the right direction. Schools sometimes call these plans individual behaviour plans (IBPs), but they also go by other names! It doesn't matter what you call it – what matters is that it is timely and based on clear evidence, and that the teaching of the skills needed is actually done. Then, of course, it needs evaluation! The responsibility for this lies with the class teacher.

After a period of time and carefully planned and targeted interventions, the school – together with the child's parents – may decide to apply for an Education, Health and Care Plan.

Think and reflect

Are children with behavioural needs also likely to have social, emotional and mental health needs?

Do you know how to write effective targets and evaluate them?

15

The Importance of Having a Plan When It All Goes Wrong

Imagine your worst-case scenario. What is the very worst thing that could happen to you in your classroom or around the school building concerning a child not behaving as you would ideally like? Is it somebody turning tables over, running amok and swearing at you? Is it something else? Perhaps something so awful that it is almost outside of the realms of possibility! Even though you may be sure this would never happen, it is extremely important to consider. Make a plan. Talk through the plan with a colleague. Now you will never be caught without a plan! The importance of this is to ensure adults don't react emotionally in the worst-case-scenario situation. This is crucial. Their emotions do not come into play; they just follow the plan. Unwanted behaviours are often emotive and can push buttons. By planning for them, we take away the element of surprise, take the adult's shock and emotion out of the situation, and whatever follows is far calmer, more reasoned and logical. No matter what age children you teach and in what context you work, you must have a plan so that things have a better chance of being dealt with calmly and rationally.

If you are a class teacher, your plan cannot be 'get the headteacher'! It has to be your own plan. What are you actually going to do? How will you behave? What sort of things might you say? The final stages of your plan – when all is exploding around you (which obviously will not happen as the earlier stages of your plan will have worked so well!) – may well be to summon help; however, there need to be stages in your own plan before this. Don't get caught with your plans down!

16

Supports for School Staff

Nobody would deny that some children can be extremely challenging. These children never seem to have a day off either! But maybe these are the children who need you, need to be in school and need security, predictability and attention. They aren't going to go away, so it is important to look at what supports can be made available to staff.

- A good whole-school behaviour policy and clear systems within it can be a huge help as it is the context within which you operate.

- Supportive staff relationships and a 'no blame' culture help staff not to feel alone.

- Whole-school preventative strategies can make it better for everyone.

- A good knowledge of specific strategies enables staff to implement and evaluate them, so staff training is important.

- An understanding of child development and current thinking can be invaluable, no matter what the age of the children in your class.

- A knowledgeable SENDCO who has time to support you is worth their weight in pencils.

- A headteacher who you know will support you if the going gets tough is a shining star!

17

Ten Very Important Things to Remember

1 None of us are perfect.

2 Behaviour can be taught; it's a skill.

3 Children develop at different rates.

4 Chronological age is not necessarily the same as emotional age.

5 Children thrive on positive relationships.

6 Adults' perceptions of 'appropriate' behaviour vary.

7 Behaviour is situational – the context can be altered.

8 It is necessary to have clear plans based on firm foundations in order to develop social, emotional and behavioural skills.

9 Children's behaviour is often not personal to the adults who live with or work with them.

10 Tomorrow is another day.

Promoting positive behaviour within primary schools can be challenging at times. Staff support individuals, all of whom are different, and the context of each school is different, so there are no definitive answers.

This book sets out some brief strategies and areas to consider in the hope that they are practical and useful. The ability to see behaviour as a set of skills which need to be taught within a context is a great help, as is the ability to focus on the positive and to see tomorrow as another day.

Index